About me

My birthday: ---

Where I live: ---

The language(s) I speak at home: --

The language(s) I'm learning: ---

Write some sentences in the languages you know here.

Language: ---------------------------------------

Language: ---------------------------------------

Language: ---------------------------------------

Great!

Wow!

1

My language skills

reading	writing	speaking	listening

1 Write the word in the spaces below.

(ear)	-------------------------------	:)
(book)	_reading_	:)
(lips)	-------------------------------	:)
(pen)	-------------------------------	:)

2 Do you like doing these things in English? Colour the faces.
Yellow = It's fantastic. Blue = It's good. Green = It's okay.

2

I can ...

Units 1-2

1 Listen. What's Stella doing? Tick the boxes.

2 Say. This is Suzy's family. Who are they?

3 Read about the Star family's house.
What do you think? Yes (✓) or no (✗)?

a   The Stars live in a small house.

b   There's an upstairs and downstairs.

c   They've got a big garden.

d   The bedrooms are downstairs.

e   They haven't got a lift.

4 Write about your home.

1

2

3

4

I can ...

Units 3–4

1 Listen and draw. What time is it?

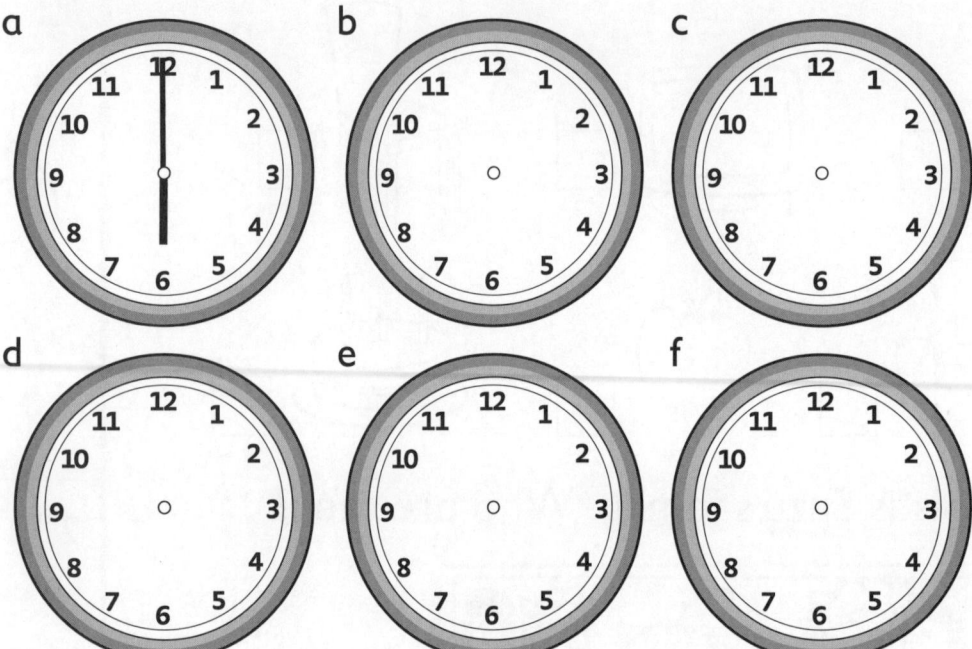

a   b   c

d   e   f

1

2 Talk about your school day.

I wake up at 7 o'clock. I eat breakfast at …

2

3 Read and write the place.

a   You can fly a kite here. _____
b   You can buy CDs here. _____
c   You can get some money here. _____
d   You go here to catch a bus. _____
e   You can eat lunch or dinner here. _____
f   You go here to find a book. _____
g   You go here to swim. _____

3

4 Write about your favourite shop. What's it called? What can you buy there?

_____

_____

_____

4

I can ...

Units 5-6

Colour the faces: I can do it!

1 🎧 Listen and point.

1

☺

2 💬 Say. What's good for you?

I go to sleep at …
I wake up at …
I play …
I like eating …

2

☺

3 🔍 Read and draw.

In the middle of the picture there's a river. There's a field in front of the river and a forest behind it. Two people are having a picnic in the field. A boy's swimming in the river. There are flowers in the field.

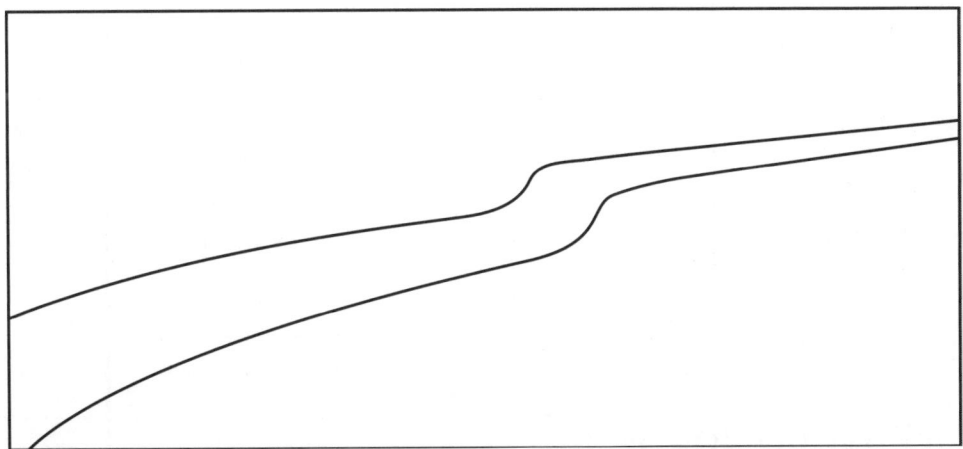

3

☺

4 ✏️ Write about you. Use four adjectives.

I'm _____

_____

_____

4 ☺

I can ...

Units 7–8

1    Listen to the descriptions and point to the animal.

2   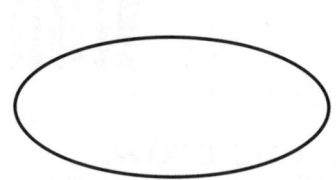 Say. Look at the pictures of the animals above.
Describe them to your partner.
Take turns.

> This animal is very big. It's bigger than a bat. It lives in the ...

3   Read and draw.

It's cold today. It's raining and very windy. I'm wearing a hat and a scarf. I'm not happy. I want to go home and drink hot chocolate!

4    Write. What do you wear?

When it's hot I wear _____

When it's cold _____

Now I'm wearing _____

6

Learning English

1   I listen to English songs:

a lot	sometimes	never

2   I read books in English:

a lot	sometimes	never

3   I watch films in English:

a lot	sometimes	never

How are you?

4   I speak to people in English:

a lot	sometimes	never

5   I have been to these places:

------------------------   ------------------------

------------------------   ------------------------

------------------------   ------------------------

6   I spoke to people in English there:

a lot	sometimes	never

World of Animals

My family

Draw or stick a picture of your family doing something you like to do together.

Who's in your picture? ---

What are you doing? --

My home

Draw or stick a picture of your house or flat.

My home is in:

the city ☐   a town ☐   the country ☐

My favourite room is _____ because I can

_____

My house has got _____

_____

9

My school day

What do you do in the morning, the afternoon and the evening on the days you go to school?
Draw pictures and write sentences.

1 I wake up at -------------------	2 ------------------- -------------------	3 ------------------- -------------------
4 ------------------- -------------------	5 ------------------- -------------------	6 ------------------- -------------------

My favourite day of the week is -------------------------------------
because ---

Being healthy

Draw or stick a picture of you doing something healthy.

Circle 'yes' or 'no'. Answer the questions.

1   I drink water: **yes** / **no**. How many glasses? _____

2   I eat fruit and vegetables: **yes** / **no**. What's your favourite fruit? _____
_____ . What's your favourite vegetable? _____ .

3   I exercise: **yes** / **no**. What sports do you like? _____ .

4   I like sleeping: **yes** / **no.** How many hours do you sleep? _____

Outside

Draw or stick a picture of you outside in your favourite place. Is it a park? Is it the beach or the mountains? Is there a river, the sea or a lake? What animals can you see?

Where are you? _____

What can you do here? _____

What can you see here? _____

_____

_____

A weather report

Look outside. What can you see? Draw your picture.
Add a thermometer. Is it cold or hot today?

What's the weather like today? _____
_____

My favourite weather is _____
_____

13

Second Edition

Kid's Box 3
Language Portfolio

This Language Portfolio allows your pupils to build a record of their progress through the school year.

The content follows the units of **Kid's Box** and the structure corresponds to that outlined by the Council of Europe's European Language Portfolio.

Please visit our website to download the Language Portfolio teaching notes.

www.cambridge.org/kidsbox

CAMBRIDGE
UNIVERSITY PRESS
www.cambridge.org

ISBN 978-1-107-64380-2

9 781107 643802 >